THE GARDEN

TRADITIONAL WOODWORKING

THE GARDEN

Step-by-step projects
for the woodworker

Watson-Guptill Publications/New York

First published in the United States by Watson-Guptill Publications,
a division of BPI Communications, Inc.,
1515 Broadway, New York, N. Y. 10036

Originally published by Collins & Brown Ltd,
London House, Great Eastern Wharf,
Parkgate Road, London SW11 4NQ

ISBN 0 8230 5401 2

Library of Congress Catalog Card Number : 97-62556

Series Editor: Liz Dean
Project Editor: Ian Kearey
Editorial Assistant: Lisa Balkwill
Designer: Suzanne Metcalfe-Megginson
Illustrator: Keith Field

Editorial Director: Sarah Hoggett
Art Director: Roger Bristow

Printed in China

First printing, 1998

1 2 3 4 5 6 7 8 9 / 06 05 04 03 02 01 00 99 98

CONTENTS

INTRODUCTION

THE PROFESSIONAL AND AMATEUR furniture makers who designed and created these projects were selected for their classic and timeless designs, high-quality craftsmanship, innovative techniques, and, not least, the ability to explain precisely how their pieces can be made. These inspiring projects are designed to suit a range of woodworking skills, from intermediate to advanced, and with their clear and detailed instructions, step-by-step photographs, and color exploded diagrams, they are well within the grasp of all enthusiastic woodworkers.

When thinking about furniture for the home, the garden is, unfortunately, rarely high on the list of priorities. As a result, even the most beautifully cultivated gardens are all too often littered with white plastic furniture that yellows with age and needs securing with a heavy object against the slightest summer's breeze. You wouldn't dream of using this furniture in your house, so why put it in your garden?

In presenting these twelve garden projects, we have tried to cover every aspect of outdoor garden life. For the gardener we have included accessories such as the Garden Trug (p. 26), a Foldaway Herb Planter for the greenhouse (p. 60), and three other types of planter designs. For larger garden equipment, wood-workers can attempt to make the Pine Arbor (p. 42) or Garden Shed (p. 36) – a great test of carpentry skills. For those who prefer to lounge rather than labor, we have a selection of seats, benches, and tables such as the Stowaway Picnic Table (p. 68).

Tools and Materials

Many of these projects require less finely detailed work than those for the living room or dining room, yet a good basic set of hand tools, well sharpened and maintained, is essential. Power tools such as a drill, jigsaw, router, and sander are extremely useful for the more tedious jobs involved, although most of the projects here can be made using hand tools only.

The timber for outdoor projects has to be chosen more carefully than for indoor projects, for obvious reasons. In every case, the primary considerations are resistance to rot and insect infestation and local availability (which will, in turn, affect the price). Certain widely available domestic hardwoods are extremely well suited to outdoor uses. Teak, which is grown in the South, and white oak, which is more or less ubiquitous, are both excellent choices. Pressure-treated pine — a softwood treated with chemical compounds to make it less appealing to fungus and insects — can be used for virtually any outdoor application; however, because the substances with which it is impregnated are potentially hazardous, it should be avoided for projects such as seating and tables. North American softwoods suitable for outdoor applications are cedar and redwood. There are some imported woods that work well in this capacity, but their cost can be prohibitive.

Although no finish can prevent decay altogether, and all finishes

LEFT: *This stow-away picnic table (p. 68) has a simple yet effective design and can be easily dismantled during the winter months.*

need to be renewed every few years, a well-chosen one will protect wood from exposure to the elements. This step is particularly important for projects that will become permanent outdoor fixtures, like the Garden Shed, Pine Arbor, and Birdhouse.

Finishing

When weatherproofing outdoor furniture, remember that you must protect not only from rain, but also from sunlight and fungus. Moisture will not only split timber but make it susceptible to biological attack, while sunlight will bleach exposed timber and degrade the surface.

There are now many products on the market that are perfect for finishing and treating outdoor timber, from natural-looking woodstains and varnishes, to durable waterproof coatings in bright primary colors, to products made specifically to treat rough-sawn wood. The good news is that many are now environmentally safe. With the proper application of the right preservative, varnish, stain, or paint, and regular maintenance, your garden furniture should enjoy a long and useful life. To help you with the finishing process, we have included a section at the back of this book about weatherproofing outdoor timber (pp. 74–77).

Most gardens, whether large or small, will be enhanced by any one of these projects. Each will give you an opportunity to express your creativity and enrich your enjoyment of your home's outdoor environment.

RIGHT: *This classic garden trug (p. 26) is a useful addition to any garden.*

VERSAILLES PLANTER

*The traditional Versailles planter
is an attractive addition to any garden,
and can be made from any hardwood or
softwood. This version has two panels on the
long side, but you can easily change the
measurements to make a square example
(see p. 48 for one of these).*

The panels on the planter slot neatly
into grooves in the rails and legs.

1 Plane the four leg sections square using a power planer and finish off with a bench plane. The finished size is 2¼ in (55 mm) square and 1 ft 6¼ in (465 mm) long, but leave the legs about ¾ in (19 mm) overlong as they will be beveled at a later stage. Using a try square, carefully check the squareness of each leg.

2 Mark the positions of the top and bottom mortises. Clamp together as shown, using a try square to mark all the faces. The bottom of the lower mortise and the top of the upper one are 2¾ in (70 mm) from the base and top of the leg respectively. The combined width of the rails and side panels is 1 ft ⅜ in (315 mm).

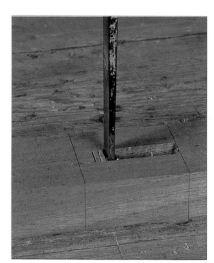  

3 Chop out 5/16-in (8-mm) wide mortises in two sides of each leg. These will intersect in the middle of the timber. Make a ⅜-in (10-mm) deep groove between the mortise openings to take the panels, using a router and ¼-in (6-mm) straight bit.

4 To give the frame joints of the planter added strength and greater durability, bore holes through the mortises. These holes need to penetrate the rear face of the mortises by only about ⅜ in (10 mm).

5 You can shape the tops of the legs into finials or roundels, but for simplicity cut a bevel of about 15° by hand or using a chop saw. Then sand down the legs – it is difficult to reach the inner surfaces of the legs once the frame of the planter is assembled.

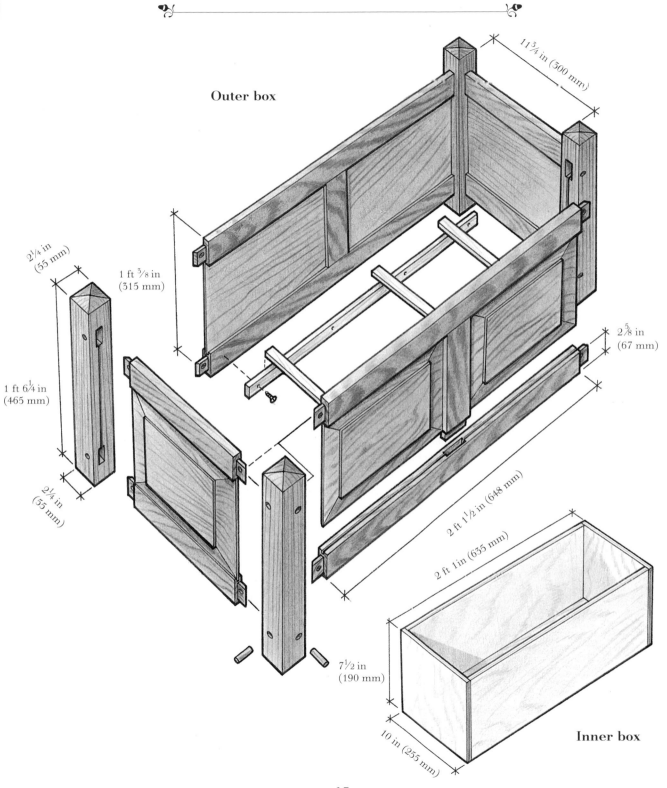

Outer box

$11\frac{3}{4}$ in (300 mm)

$2\frac{1}{4}$ in (55 mm)

1 ft $\frac{3}{8}$ in (315 mm)

1 ft $6\frac{1}{4}$ in (465 mm)

$2\frac{1}{4}$ in (55 mm)

$2\frac{5}{8}$ in (67 mm)

2 ft $1\frac{1}{2}$ in (648 mm)

2 ft 1 in (635 mm)

$7\frac{1}{2}$ in (190 mm)

10 in (255 mm)

Inner box

6 Cut the long side rails to 2 ft 4 in (710 mm) long, including 1⅛ in (30 mm) tenons each end. Cut the short end rails to 1 ft 2¼ in (360 mm) length. You can start the cuts for the tenons by hand while using a vice to keep the wood at 45° to the bench.

7 Next, reverse the wood and cut at the same angle from the other side before cutting directly down on the tenon. Finish off the tenons with a back saw and bench hook. As the tenons will meet in the center of each leg, miter the ends to 45°.

8 Cut two central divisions to 1 ft 3¼ in (385 mm). Mark the mortise positions on each rail and cut the center pieces' tenons as in Steps 6–7. Router grooves for the panels on the inner edge of each rail using a ¼ in (6 mm) straight cutter.

9 Cut the panels, then clear the waste. Finally, use hand planes or a spindle shaper to cut a rabbet of 1¾ in (45 mm) around the edge.

10 Test-fit all the components together using a rubber mallet, ensuring that all the pieces fit together snugly. Then make any last adjustments as necessary.

11 Place the drill bit in the mortise-and-tenon of a leg, marking the tenon. Next, take the joint apart and drill the tenon ⅛ in (4 mm) inboard of the drill mark, nearer the tenon shoulder as shown. Then drill similar holes in the mortises and the tenons of the other legs.

12 Use a waterproof glue to assemble the two ends and two long sides of the planter. Check that all sections are square using a try square. Assemble the complete planter and peg the joints, adding a touch of glue to each peg and cutting off the piece that protrudes. Sand smooth.

LIST OF MATERIALS (*measurements indicate cut size*)		
ITEM	SECTION	LENGTH
Hardwood/treated softwood for legs, 4	2¼ x 2¼ in (55 x 55 mm)	6 ft 4 in (1963 mm)
Hardwood/treated softwood for rails, 8 and central divisions, 2	2⅝ x ⅞ in (67 x 21 mm)	16 ft 7½ in (5050 mm)
Plywood for panels, 6	8¾ x ¾ or ⅜ in (220 x 19 or 10 mm)	5 ft 10½ in (1800 mm)
Hardwood pegs		
Woodscrews		

Making an Inner Box

An inner box is used to protect the life of the planter. To construct an inner box, use ⅝ or ¾ in (15 or 19 mm) exterior-grade plywood, cut to around 1⅝ in (40 mm) undersize on all sides. Biscuit joints are ideal for holding the four sides and base together. To support the box, screw a ¾ x 1⅜ in (19 x 35 mm) bearer to the bottom rail of each long side of the planter, and then rest three further bearers across it.

BIRDHOUSE

*This traditional birdhouse design has been adapted to make an unusual
and decorative nesting box for small garden birds. It is made entirely
from plywood and uses no joints in its construction.*

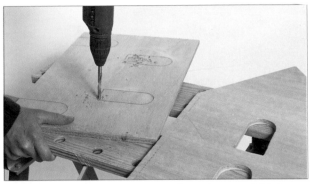

1 Mark and cut out the sides to 1 ft 6 in (460 mm)
length and 1 ft (305 mm) width. Cut ends and partition to 1 ft 8 in (510 mm) length and 1 ft (305 mm)
width, then mark from the center at the top to 1 ft
(305 mm) from the bottom at the sides of all three pieces.
Cut away the waste, saving it for the ledge supports, and
check that the roof pitch matches.

2 The false entrance holes are 4½ in (115 mm) high
and 2 in (50 mm) wide, with an arched top. Mark out
four holes in each side piece, two level with the bottom
and positioned 2 in (50 mm) from the side edges, and two
with their bases 6 in (150 mm) above the bottom and 5 in
(125 mm) from the side edges. Drill a ⅜ in (10 mm) hole
in the corner of each of the higher entrance holes.

3 Cut out all the arched recesses
on both side pieces. On both end
pieces, mark out one false entrance
hole level with the bottom and
positioned centrally, and cut it out.
On the back end piece only, mark out
another false entrance hole positioned directly
above the lower one, with its base
6 in (150 mm) from the bottom. Drill
a corner hole and cut out as before.

4 The real entrance hole is placed
centrally above the false entrance
hole on the front end piece. With
the metal end of a pair of compasses
positioned 9 in (230 mm) from the
end bottom, mark a 1½ in (38 mm)
diameter hole. Drill a ⅜ in (10 mm)
hole and cut out the entrance hole
with a coping saw or a narrow scroll
blade in a jigsaw. Sand the edges.

5 To assemble the sides, front and
back, glue the vertical edges
of the sides and nail them in place,
butting up to the inner face of the
front and back. Check all the corners
for square, and set aside to dry.

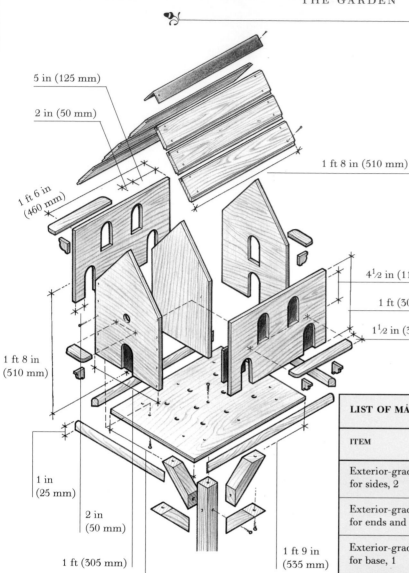

5 in (125 mm)

2 in (50 mm)

1 ft 8 in (510 mm)

1 ft 6 in (460 mm)

4½ in (115 mm)

1 ft (305 mm)

1½ in (38 mm)

1 ft 8 in (510 mm)

1 in (25 mm)

2 in (50 mm)

1 ft (305 mm)

1 ft 2 in (356 mm)

1 ft 9 in (535 mm)

Making a Post

For protection, the box should be at least 7 ft (2140 mm) above the ground, and should be sheltered from midday sun and prevailing winds. To make a post, cut 8 ft 6 in (2595 mm) length from 2 in (50 mm) square timber, and screw four mitered bracing pieces of the same square section to each side and the birdhouse base. Treat the post with preservative, and either set it with mortar and rubble in a 1 ft 6 in (460 mm) hole, or secure it with a metal post anchor.

LIST OF MATERIALS (*measurements indicate cut size*)		
ITEM	**SECTION**	**LENGTH**
Exterior-grade plywood for sides, 2	1 ft x ½ in (305 x 12 mm)	3 ft (920 mm)
Exterior-grade plywood for ends and partition, 3	1 ft x ½ in (305 x 12 mm)	5 ft (1530 mm)
Exterior-grade plywood for base, 1	1ft 2 in x ½ in (356 x 12 mm)	1 ft 9 in (535 mm)
Exterior-grade plywood for ledges, 4	1¼ x ½ in (32 x 12 mm)	2 ft (610 mm)
Exterior-grade plywood scraps for ledge supports, 6	1 x ½ in (25 x 12 mm)	1 ft 6in (460 mm)
Tongue-and-groove cladding for roof pieces, 6	4 x ½ in (100 x 12 mm)	10 ft (3060 mm)
Softwood edge molding	1 in (25 mm)	7 ft (2140 mm)
Asphalt damp-proof tape		
Panel nails	1¼ in (32 mm)	

6 Glue the vertical edges of the partition, position it about 4 in (100 mm) from the front end piece, and nail it in place to form two internal "boxes."

7 Cut six 1 ft 8 in (510 mm) lengths of tongue-and-groove cladding and pin them on to the sloping edges of the end pieces and partition, starting from the top and leaving a 1 in (25 mm) overhang at the front and back.

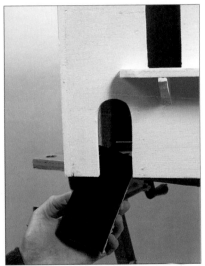

8 Mark out the decorative ledges from plywood. Cut the side ledges 9 in (230 mm) long and the end ledges 3 in (75 mm) long, and round the ends. Position the side and back end ledges level with the bottom of the higher arched recesses, and glue in place. Position the front end ledge 1 in (25 mm) centrally below the circular entrance hole, and glue in place. Shape two supports for each side ledge and one for each end ledge, then glue in place.

9 Apply a water-based preservative or white paint to the whole birdhouse. Nail a strip of asphalt damp-proof tape along the roof ridge. To give the appearance of open arched entrances, cut ten pieces of scrap plywood larger than the false recesses, paint them with black exterior paint, and glue them to the back of each recess.

10 Cut a 1 ft 9 in (535 mm) length of 1 ft 2 in x ½ in (356 x 12 mm) plywood for the base. Cut appropriate lengths of 1 in (25 mm) molding and miter the corners, then glue and pin the molding to the base edges. Place the birdhouse centrally on the base, mark and drill screw holes on the base, and screw the birdhouse and base together. (Using screws, the birdhouse can be opened up and cleaned.) Drill several 1 in (25 mm) holes in the base for water drainage.

OCTAGONAL TABLE

This handsome table is made from common timber stock sizes, and either hardwood or treated softwood can be used in its construction. The design can be adapted to make four or six sides, or even a circular top, using a trammel and router.

The table's four cross braces use central halving joints to ensure a neat fit.

1 Plane each leg to 2⁷⁄₈ in (72 mm) square, and cut them to 2 ft 2¼ in (665 mm) long. Clamp the legs together and mark for the bottom cross brace mortises 4 in (100 mm) from the bottom of each leg.

2 Then cut ¾-in (19-mm) deep tenons, which is one-third of the timber width, on the top of each leg. You can number or mark each leg to make the assembly easier.

3 Use a chisel to chop out mortises 2 in (50 mm) wide and 1¾ in (45 mm) deep for the cross braces at the bottom of each leg. Drawbore ⅜ in (10 mm) dowel holes through the middle of each mortise.

4 Plane the four cross braces to 2 x 2⁷⁄₈ in (50 x 72 mm) and cut the bottom pair 2 ft 3½ in (700 mm) long. Using a marking gauge and try square, mark the central halving joint on each brace, cross-cut the sections of the joint and chisel out the waste. Level the bottom of the joints and check the fit. Cut a 2 x 1¾ in (50 x 45 mm) tenon on each end of the bottom braces.

5 Cut the top cross braces to 2 ft 10¾ in (880 mm) long. Using a cardboard template, mark out a 2 in (50 mm) curve at the ends of each brace, then cut the curves with a bandsaw. Cut mortises on the end of each brace so that they fit the tenons on the tops of all four legs.

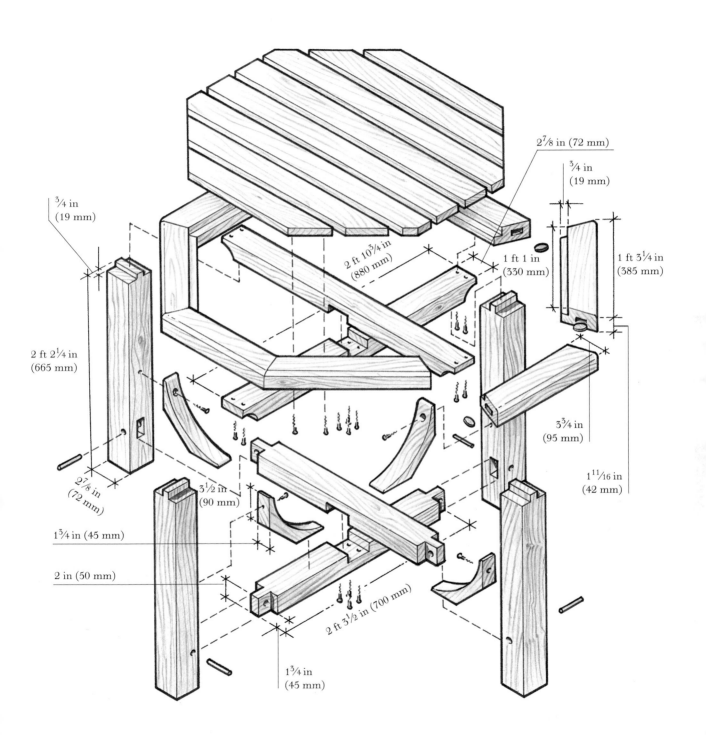

2⁷⁄8 in (72 mm)

³⁄4 in (19 mm)

1 ft 3¹⁄4 in (385 mm)

³⁄4 in (19 mm)

2 ft 10³⁄4 in (880 mm)

1 ft 1 in (330 mm)

2 ft 2¹⁄4 in (665 mm)

3³⁄4 in (95 mm)

2⁷⁄8 in (72 mm)

1¹¹⁄16 in (42 mm)

3¹⁄2 in (90 mm)

1³⁄4 in (45 mm)

2 in (50 mm)

2 ft 3¹⁄2 in (700 mm)

1³⁄4 in (45 mm)

6 Drill four screw holes in the halving joints of the bottom cross braces, and glue and screw together. Dry-assemble the legs and cross braces, checking that the parts fit together. Using the drilled holes in the legs as guides, drill dowel holes through the tenons in the cross braces.

7 Glue all the joints and reassemble the legs and cross braces. Glue and hammer in dowels through the legs and bottom braces, using a rubber mallet or a wooden one with a piece of scrap softwood beneath, and hammer home the top leg tenons and top cross brace mortises.

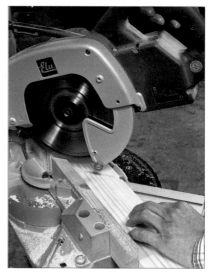

8 Cut four decorative knees to about 1 ft (305 mm) length. Use a card template to mark out their shape, and then cut the knees to shape on a bandsaw. Glue the knees to the legs and bottom cross braces, or drill countersunk holes and screw together.

9 For the top sections, make up full-size MDF templates, 3¾ in (95 mm) wide, 1 ft 1 in (330 mm) long on the inner face and 1 ft 3¼ in (385 mm) long on outer face. Trace onto 1¹¹⁄₁₆-in (42-mm) thick planed softwood, and cut on a miter saw.

10 Rabbet the inner face of each section by ¾ in (19 mm) to take the top slats. This procedure will enable you to cut each piece with accuracy, either by using a chop saw or cutting by hand.

11 Using a biscuit joiner, cut two slots in the ends of each top section, or alternatively cut plywood biscuits on a bandsaw and then cut slots for them with a router. Glue and fit the biscuits, then glue up and assemble the table top, clamping it using a web clamp and eight softwood corners cut to fit around each angle.

12 Mark the positions of eight slats on the top section rabbet, spacing them 1 in (25 mm) apart. Cut and plane the slats to length; check that they are symmetrical. Drill two holes for each slat end in the rabbet, and two screw holes in the end of each top cross brace. Screw the top section to the top cross braces, and the slats to the top.

LIST OF MATERIALS (*measurements indicate cut size*)		
ITEM	SECTION	LENGTH
Hardwood/treated softwood for legs, 4	$2^7/8$ x $2^7/8$ in (72 x 72 mm)	8 ft 9 in (2660 mm)
Hardwood/treated softwood for cross braces, 4	2 x $2^7/8$ in (50 x 72 mm)	10 ft $4^1/2$ in (3160 mm)
Hardwood/treated softwood for top sections, 8	$1^{11}/16$ x $3^3/4$ in (42 x 95 mm)	10 ft 2 in (3080 mm)
Hardwood/treated softwood for top slats, 8	$1^1/16$ x 3 in (27 x 75 mm)	19 ft 6 in (6000 mm)
Hardwood/treated softwood for knees, 4	$1^3/4$ x $3^1/2$ in (45 x 90 mm)	4 ft (1220 mm)
Softwood dowels, 4	$3/8$ in (10 mm) diameter	
Woodscrews, 56		

GARDEN TRUG

Traditionally, garden trugs come in all sizes and can be square or rounded
at the ends. This useful shallow carrier can be constructed from sound offcuts
of hardwood or softwood; beech can be bent easily for the handle.

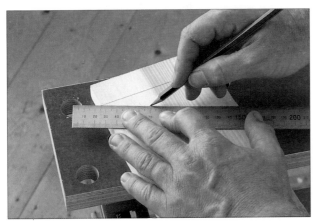

1 Mark out and cut the sides to 1 ft 4 in (406 mm) lengths and the ends to 8 in (200 mm) lengths. Mark the sides 2 in (50 mm) in from the bottom edges, draw a line to each top corner, and cut along the lines. Follow the same procedure on the ends, marking the lines 1 in (25 mm) in from the bottom edges.

2 The ends fit inside the sides. Mark the angles required and cut them. Mark the angles on a piece of scrap wood; this will be used to mark out the bottom. Drill three small nail holes at each end of the sides. Chamfer off the inside edge of the top faces of the ends as shown to about ¼ in (6 mm), to reduce the thickness and match the sides.

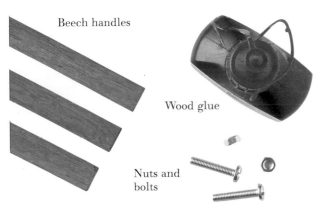

Beech handles

Wood glue

Nuts and bolts

3 Apply glue to the edges of the ends, and nail one side in position. Turn the work over and nail on the other side. Mark and cut two or more 2 ft (610 mm) lengths of ¾ x ⅛ in (19 x 4 mm) timber, preferably beech, for the handle. It is a good idea to make a number of these, as steam-bending wood is often a trial-and-error operation.

4 Partly fill a large aluminum pot with water, and heat it through until it boils. Carefully place one end of the handle into the boiling water, remove it and, wearing protective gloves, hold it under pressure until it starts to bend. Swap ends and exert pressure again, repeating until the rough shape is achieved.

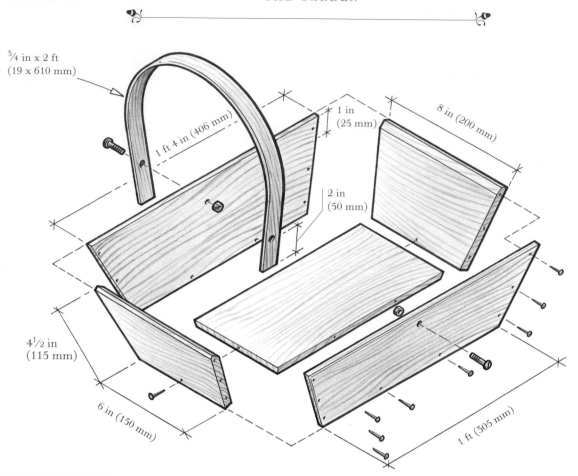

¾ in x 2 ft
(19 x 610 mm)

1 ft 4 in (406 mm)

1 in
(25 mm)

8 in (200 mm)

2 in
(50 mm)

4½ in
(115 mm)

6 in (150 mm)

1 ft (305 mm)

LIST OF MATERIALS (*measurements indicate cut size*)		
ITEM	SECTION	LENGTH
Hardwood/softwood for sides, 2	4½ x ¼ in (115 x 6 mm)	2 ft 8 in (810 mm)
Hardwood/softwood for ends, 2	4½ x ½ in (115 x 12 mm)	1ft 4 in (406 mm)
Hardwood/softwood for bottom, 1	6 x ⅜ in (150 x 10 mm)	1 ft (305 mm)
Hardwood/softwood for handle, 1	¾ x ⅛ in (19 x 4 mm)	2 ft (610 mm)
Nuts and bolts, 2	¼ in (6 mm) diameter	
Copper/brass nails		

5 Make up a former to hold the handles in the required shape. Place each handle end into the boiling water to soften them, and then insert them immediately into the former and let dry. Don't attempt to fit the handle to the frame until it is completely dry, or it may pull the sides out of shape.

6 Mark out and cut a 1 ft (305 mm) length of timber for the bottom. Mark out and bevel the edges to give a tight fit in the frame, at least $1/8$ in (4 mm) from the base edges. Check the fit, apply glue, push it in tight and drill for nail holes, two through each side and one through each end. Nail the bottom in place.

7 Mark a central hole 2 in (50 mm) from each end of the handle, and drill, using a $1/4$ in (6 mm) bit. Mark a corresponding central hole 1 in (25 mm) down from the top edge of each side, and drill the holes.

8 Apply glue under the ends of the handle, and fit the handle in place using nuts and bolts. With the nuts tight, cut the ends off the bolts on the inside, and use a center punch to tap a dent into the edge of each nut and bolt to hold the nut in place.

BENCH-AND-TABLE SET

*This solidly constructed bench-and-table set can make an attractive focal
point in any garden. You can use hardwood or softwood, staining as
required, and the project uses mortise-and-tenon and dowel joints.*

1 Cut the bench back rail to 3 ft 10¾ in (1190 mm),
shape the curve to 2 in (50 mm) at the ends, then tenon
the ends. Cut the back seat rail to the same length, angle
the upper face by 14°, and add two ½ in (12 mm) dowels
at each end. Cut the nine backrest slats to 1 ft 3⅜ in
(390 mm), and tenon each end. Mark and cut nine
mortises in the large back rail, and nine in the back seat
rail, using wedges to align the rail so that the sloping top
is at right angles to the chisel. Dry-assemble the back.

2 Cut the two back leg pieces to 1 ft 6 in (460 mm), and
angle the tops to 28°. Cut two sloping back leg pieces
square to 1 ft 8 in (510 mm), then mark a 14° angle. Use
the lower leg pieces to mark very carefully a bird's mouth
V-joint on the upper piece. Clean up both pieces, and then
glue and clamp up the legs. When dry, drill dowel holes to
take the back seat rail dowels, and mortise to take the two
side rails and large back rail.

3 Mark and cut the front legs to 1 ft 11½ in (598 mm).
Cut tenons at the top for the armrests, and then the
mortises for the front and side rails. Cut the two side rails
to 1 ft 8 in (510 mm) and the long front rail to 3 ft 10¾ in
(1190 mm), then shape them as for the bench back rail
(see Step 1), and cut tenons.

4 Cut the center support strut to 1 ft 6 in (460 mm),
add two dowels at each end, then drill the front and
back seat rails for dowels. Cut the armrests to 2 ft 1¾ in
(650 mm), then mortise the front undersides for the leg
tenons. Cut a 14° angle on the rear edge to match the back
angle, and add dowels. Dry-assemble the frame.

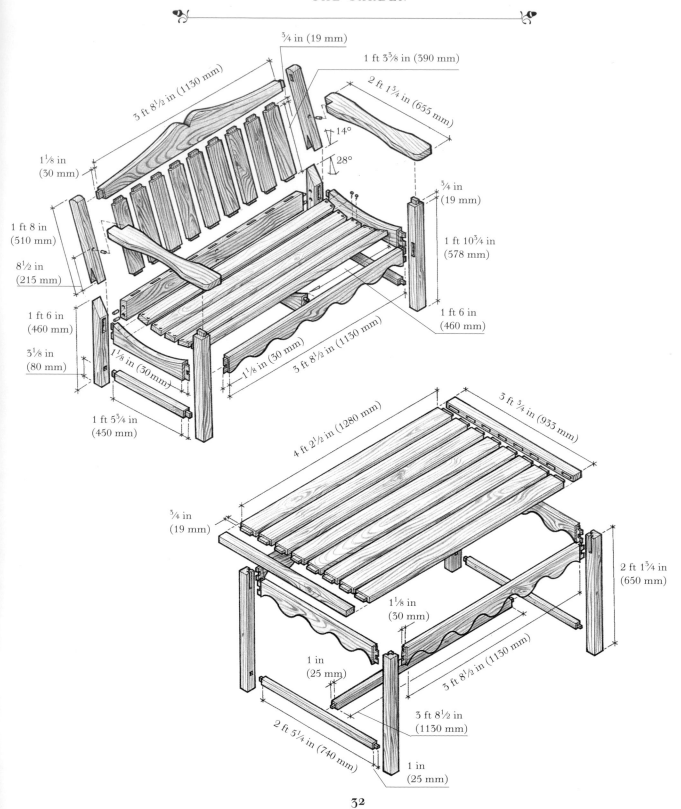

¾ in (19 mm)

1 ft 3⅜ in (390 mm)

2 ft 1¾ in (655 mm)

3 ft 8½ in (1130 mm)

14°

28°

1⅛ in (30 mm)

¾ in (19 mm)

1 ft 8 in (510 mm)

1 ft 10¾ in (578 mm)

8½ in (215 mm)

1 ft 6 in (460 mm)

1 ft 6 in (460 mm)

3⅛ in (80 mm)

1⅛ in (30 mm)

1⅛ in (30 mm)

3 ft 8½ in (1130 mm)

1 ft 5¾ in (450 mm)

4 ft 2½ in (1280 mm)

3 ft ¾ in (933 mm)

¾ in (19 mm)

2 ft 1¾ in (650 mm)

1⅛ in (30 mm)

1 in (25 mm)

3 ft 8½ in (1130 mm)

2 ft 5¼ in (740 mm)

3 ft 8½ in (1130 mm)

1 in (25 mm)

5 Using the frame to check the exact length, cut the five seat slats to 4 ft (1220 mm) length, and drill the ends to take woodscrews; if you are using hardwood, countersink the holes for the screw heads. Disassemble the frame, apply glue and clamp up the whole bench.

6 For the table, mark and cut the legs to 2 ft 1¾ in (650 mm) length, then mark and cut the mortises for the four top rails and two lower rails. Cut the two long top rails to 3 ft 10¾ in (1190 mm) and the two short top rails to 2 ft 7¾ in (810 mm), tenon the ends, and use a bandsaw or jigsaw to cut the curves.

7 Cut the bottom rails to 2 ft 7¼ in (790 mm), then tenon the ends and cut a mortise in the center of each rail. Cut the bottom center rail to 3 ft 10½ in (1182 mm), and tenon each end to fit the rail mortises. Dry-assemble the table frame.

8 Check that all the joints fit and that the frame is square, then apply glue to the mortise and tenons and assemble the frame, using bar clamps to hold it.

9 Check the frame components for square at all stages, using a try square for the internal 90° angles, and ensuring that the diagonal measurements are the same on all sides.

10 With the frame assembled, cut the eight slats to 4 ft 4 in (1320 mm) length, and tenon the ends to match the closed end pieces.

11 Cut the closed end pieces to 3 ft ¾ in (933 mm) length, and mark and cut the mortises to match the slats. Dry-assemble the table top and check for square, then glue and clamp up. Let dry, then glue and fit the top to the frame.

LIST OF MATERIALS (*measurements indicate cut size*)		
BENCH	**SECTION**	**LENGTH**
Hardwood/softwood for back rail, 1	6 x 1½ in (150 x 38 mm)	3 ft 10¾ in (1190 mm)
Hardwood/softwood for back leg verticals, 2, slopes, 2, and front legs, 2	2 x 2 in (50 x 50 mm)	10 ft 3 in (3136 mm)
Hardwood/softwood for seat slats, 5	3 x 1 in (75 x 25 mm)	20 ft (6100 mm)
Hardwood/softwood for backrest slats, 9	3 x ¾ in (75 x 19 mm)	11 ft 6⅜ in (3510 mm)
Hardwood/softwood for front seat rail, 1, back seat rail, 1, side seat rails, 2, arm rests, 2, and center support strut, 1	4 x 1½ in (100 x 38 mm)	16 ft 11 in (5160 mm)
TABLE Hardwood/softwood for legs, 4	2 x 2 in (50 x 50 mm)	8 ft 7 in (2600 mm)
Hardwood/softwood for long top rails, 2, short top rails, 2, and slats, 8	4 x 1½ in (100 x 38 mm)	47 ft 9 in (14 m 560 mm)
Hardwood/softwood for closed end pieces, 2	2 x 1½ in (50 x 38 mm)	6 ft 1½ in (1870 mm)
Hardwood/softwood for bottom center rail, 1, and bottom rails, 2	1½ x 1½ in (38 x 38 mm)	9 ft 1 in (2762 mm)
Doweling	½ in (12 mm) diameter	
Woodscrews		

Assembly and Finishing

It is best to build up the bench and table in sections, applying glue to the mortise and dowel holes only. Where necessary, tap the joints together with a mallet or rubber-faced hammer. Always check frames using a try square and measure all the diagonals. Wipe away all surplus adhesive as it appears, using a damp rag.

If you intend to stain the timber, do so before assembling the bench-and-table set; otherwise, stray leaks of surplus glue may resist or repel the stain applied.

When applying protective varnish, make sure that you treat all the undersurfaces, paying particular attention to the bottoms of the legs. ·

GARDEN SHED

This shed can be adapted to any dimensions to suit the space available in your garden or yard; you can also add more windows, or have none at all. The shed uses no joints in its construction, but is screwed and nailed together.

1 Mark and cut the front and back frame components to length, including the vertical braces and the braces for the door. Drill pilot holes and screw the components together. Repeat the process for the side frames, including the window braces. Assemble and screw together the four frames, checking them for square. Cut the corner blocks to length and screw them to the frames.

2 Cut all the clapboards to length, allowing for corner stops. The number of pieces shown here allows for one window, but must be changed if you use more or none. Position the first piece of clapboard to the bottom of the frame, allowing a 1 in (25 mm) overlap beyond the bottom of the frame.

3 Add the other pieces of weatherboard, working from the bottom up and allowing a 1 in (25 mm) overlap on each one. You can make a simple marking gauge, as illustrated here, to ensure that the overlap is accurate throughout. Nail the boards in place on all four sides of the frame.

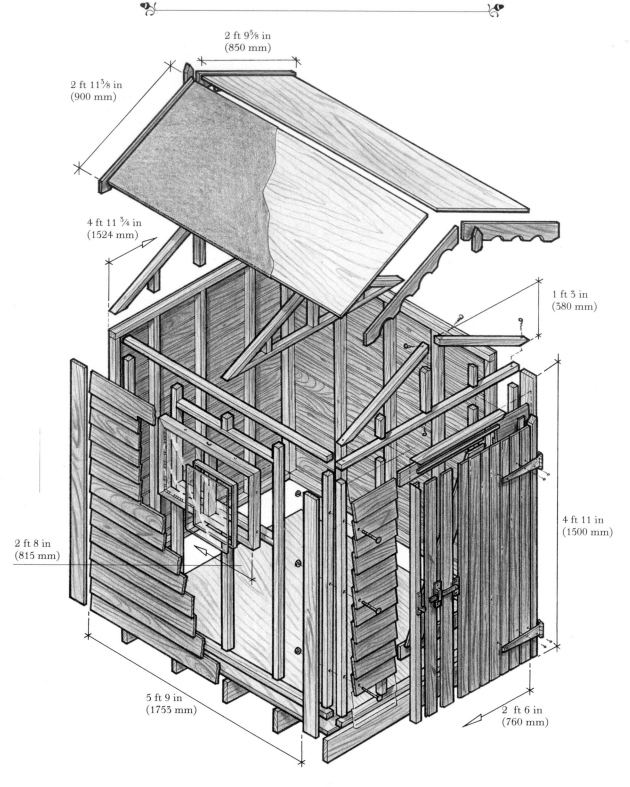

2 ft 9⅝ in
(850 mm)

2 ft 11⅜ in
(900 mm)

4 ft 11 ¾ in
(1524 mm)

1 ft 3 in
(380 mm)

2 ft 8 in
(815 mm)

4 ft 11 in
(1500 mm)

5 ft 9 in
(1753 mm)

2 ft 6 in
(760 mm)

4 Mark out the pitch of the roof full-size on a piece of plywood, and mark and cut the components for the three roof trusses, mitering them at the top. You can use horizontal braces, as shown in the photograph, or vertical ones, as shown in the diagram. Drill pilot holes and screw them to the frame, one at each end and one in the middle.

5 Cut the window and door frames to length, mitering the ends. Dry-assemble them and check for square and that they fit into their respective frames. In the window frame, mark and drill pilot holes in the middle of the top and bottom components, for the center strut.

6 Drill pilot holes and then screw the door and window frames together, including the center strut in the window frame. Position and screw them into their frames, then nail the stops inside the joins.

7 Mark and cut the tongue-and-groove boards for the door, leaving them approximately 1 in (25 mm) overlong at each end. Fit them together along their length, tapping them into place gently with a wooden or rubber mallet.

8 Mark and cut the two horizontal door ledges and diagonal door brace to length, and miter the brace to fit between the ledges. Lay the ledges and brace in position on the back of the door boards, then screw them in place. Turn the door over and nail the boards to the backing, then trim the door to fit the frame. Hang the door using two black T-hinges.

9 Cut the boards to the roof to size and nail them in place. Cut the roofing felt oversize, and tack it in place along the sides of the roof. Cut and miter two sets of barge boards, then mark decorations along the bottom edges and cut them out with a jigsaw. Tack the felt under the ends of the roof and screw the barge boards to the roof trusses over the ends of the roof.

LIST OF MATERIALS (*measurements indicate cut size*)

ITEM	SECTION	LENGTH
Softwood for front, back and side frames, 4	1¾ x 1½ in (45 x 38 mm)	147 ft 8 in (45 m)
Softwood for door and window frames, 2, roof trusses, 3, corner blocks, 4, and underfloor boards, 5	3½ x 1½ in (90 x 38 mm)	101 ft 9 in (31 m)
Softwood for barge boards, 4, door ledges, 2, and door brace, 1	6 x 1 in (150 x 25 mm)	22 ft 7½ in (6900 mm)
Softwood for door and window stops, 7	⅞ x ½ in (21 x 12 mm)	22 ft 1½ in (6750 mm)
Softwood tongue-and-groove boards for door, 9	4½ x ⅝ in (115 x 16 mm)	44 ft 4 in (13.5 m)
Softwood for clapboards, 75	6 x 1 in (150 x 25 mm)	295 ft 4 in (90 m)
Plywood for floor, 1	5 ft x ½ in (1525 x 12 mm)	5 ft 9 in (1753 mm)
Sterling board for roof, 2	5 ft 9 in x ½ in (1753 x 12 mm)	5 ft 6⅞ in (1700 mm)
Heavy-gauge asphalt roofing felt		
Size 8 woodscrews		2 in (50 mm)
Galvanized clout nails		½ in (12 mm)
Black T-hinges, 2		1 ft (305 mm)
Thumb latch and stop, 1		

Flooring and Finishing

The floor is cut to size from plywood. The shed is positioned over it (you will need strong help for this) and the floor is nailed to the bottom frame components. To prevent damp entering through the bottom, nail waterproof plastic strips over the underfloor boards. Position the boards at regular intervals on level ground, and raise the shed onto them.

The whole exterior of the shed must be weatherproofed, using one of the many exterior treatments available (see pp. 76–79). Follow the manufacturers' instructions at all times, as some of the treatments can be hazardous to health if they are not used correctly. Keep an eye on the state of the roofing felt, and be sure to replace it when it starts to deteriorate.

PINE ARBOR

*This attractive project creates a focal
point within a garden, and can provide
support for a variety of climbing plants.
It is best to select straight pieces of timber,
as this saves planing before you make
the mortise-and-tenon and
cross-halving joints.*

The braces are nailed to the frame.

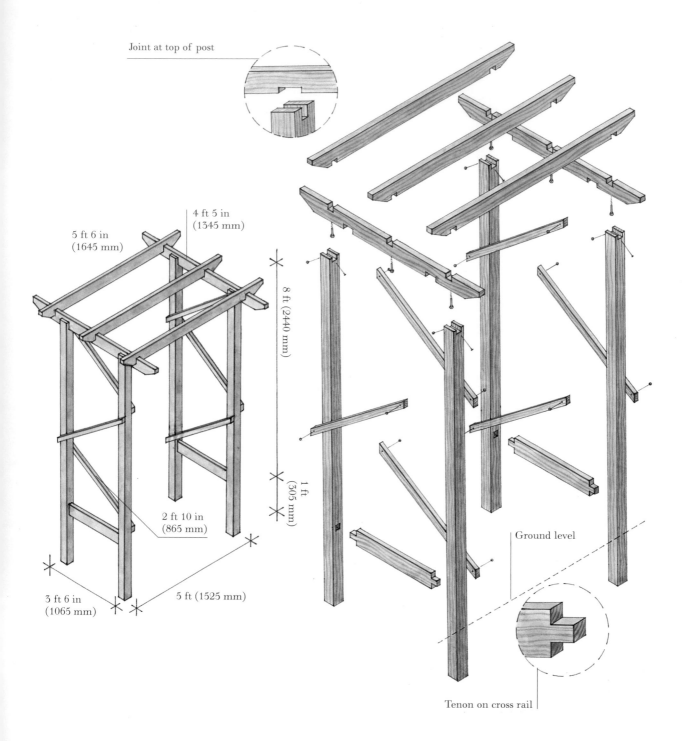

Joint at top of post

5 ft 6 in
(1645 mm)

4 ft 5 in
(1345 mm)

8 ft (2440 mm)

2 ft 10 in
(865 mm)

1 ft
(305 mm)

Ground level

3 ft 6 in
(1065 mm)

5 ft (1525 mm)

Tenon on cross rail

1 Mark out the finished lengths and joints on the various components except the braces. Use C-clamps to clamp together the components that are the same – posts together, top bearers together, and so on. Mark across them while they are clamped so that you know that the joints will all be at the same level when assembled. Mark 30° bevels on the top bearers and crosspieces, then use a mortise gauge to mark the positions for the cross rails on the posts.

2 Cut the mortises in the posts with a chisel and mallet, and make sure they are square and clean. If necessary, pare down the sides of the mortises. Next, cut the tenons on each end of the cross rails with a tenon saw (see inset).

3 Use a hand saw to cut slots in the tops of the posts and clean out with a chisel. Dry-assemble the mortise-and-tenon joints, adjust as needed, and clamp waste strips across each pair of posts. Check that the marked cross halving joints on the two top bearers correspond to the distance across the tops of the clamped-up posts. Saw out and clean the notches, making sure that the notches in the top bearers are no more than 1 in (25 mm) deep. Cut the six cross-halving joints that take the crosspieces in the upper sides of the top bearers and check for fit.

4 Saw the 30° bevels on the ends of the top components and clean up with a plane. Drill countersunk clearance holes in the undersides of the two top bearers for the screws that will hold the cross-halving joints together. Knock the joints together with a mallet, then use a bradawl to mark the pilot holes in the crosspieces.

5 Dismantle the frame and drill the pilot holes in the crosspieces. Spread waterproof glue lightly over each half of each cross-halving joint, than knock the joints back together and secure them with screws.

6 Dismantle the dry-assembled posts, spread glue on the tenons, and then reassemble the joints again. Having glued all the mortise-and-tenon joints, clamp waste strips across the tops of the posts to hold them parallel.

7 Mark the positions of the six braces on the assembled posts and cut the mitered ends of the braces in a miter box. Drill clearance holes for nails in the braces, then nail the braces in place.

LIST OF MATERIALS (*measurements indicate cut size*)		
ITEM	SECTION	LENGTH
Hardwood/softwood for posts, 4	2½ x 2½ in (65 x 65 mm)	32 ft (9760 mm)
Hardwood/softwood for cross rails, 2	4 x 1½ in (100 x 38 mm)	4 ft 6 in (1370 mm)
Hardwood/softwood for top bearers, 2	4 x 1½ in (100 x 38 mm)	8 ft 9 in (2690 mm)
Hardwood/softwood for crosspieces, 3	4 x 1½ in (100 x 38 mm)	16 ft 6 in (5025 mm)
Hardwood/softwood for braces, 6	2 x 1 in (50 x 25 mm)	17 ft (5190 mm)
No. 10 countersunk brass screws, 6		3 in (75 mm)
Nails, roundhead		2 in (50 mm)

Finishing and Using a Fence Post Spike

Using pre-treated wood is the easiest, but not the cheapest option when applying chemical preservatives to soft wood. Colored preservatives can brighten up garden furniture – to apply, brush them on or leave the ends to soak them up. With either method, pay particular attention to the end grain of the wood.

A fence post spike has a long tapering shaft with a square cup on the top. Primarily, post spikes are used to give a structure increased stability, specifically when a *precise alignment is required, as with an arbor. The shaft is driven into the ground and the base of the post is slotted into the cup.*

Depending upon the design of the spike, the fence post is secured in the cup by nails, or by tightening up a number of bolts that clamp the post rigid. Choose spikes with cups that match the size of the arbor posts. Always check that the posts are vertical before positioning the top frame and skew-nailing in place.

SQUARE PLANTER

This attractive square planter can be made from any species of solid hardwood, and provides a long-lasting alternative to earthenware pots. You can turn the decorative finials or buy them pre-turned to size.

1 Mark out and cut the $1\frac{3}{4}$ x $1\frac{3}{4}$ in (45 x 45 mm) timber to four lengths of 1 ft 6 in (460 mm) for the legs. Mark out and cut the $2\frac{3}{4}$ x $\frac{7}{8}$ in (70 x 21 mm) timber to eight lengths of 1 ft $2\frac{1}{4}$ in (360 mm) for the cross rails and four lengths of 11 in (280 mm) for the uprights. You can use $5\frac{3}{4}$ x $\frac{7}{8}$ in (145 x 21 mm) timber for the latter pieces; convert this by cutting the boards lengthways down the middle, using a circular saw, and plane to size.

2 Mark out the positions of two $2\frac{3}{4}$ x $\frac{1}{4}$ in (70 x 6 mm) mortises on adjacent sides of each leg. The upper edge of the top mortise is $1\frac{1}{8}$ in (30 mm) from the top of the leg, and the lower edge of the bottom mortise is $2\frac{3}{8}$ in (60 mm) from the leg bottom. Cut the mortise slots, using a $\frac{1}{4}$ in (6 mm) chisel or a $\frac{1}{4}$ in (6 mm) router bit, making sure that the slots are parallel.

3 Mark out $2\frac{3}{4}$ x $\frac{1}{4}$ in (70 x 6 mm) tenons on the end of each cross rail and upright, using a mortise gauge, try square and marking knife, and cut the tenons with a tenon saw held horizontally. Mark a $2\frac{3}{4}$ x $\frac{1}{4}$ in (70 x 6 mm) mortise in the middle of one edge of each of the cross rails, and cut the slot as before, ensuring that the ends of the slots are squared off.

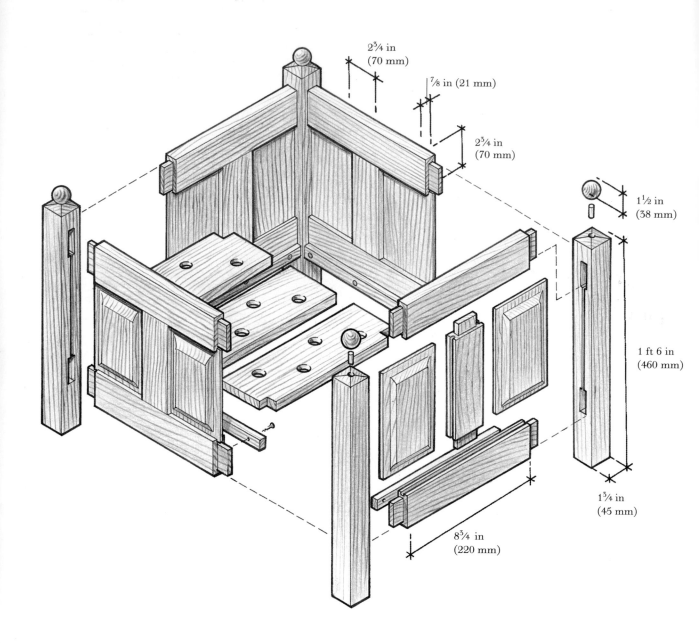

2¾ in
(70 mm)

⅞ in (21 mm)

2¾ in
(70 mm)

1½ in
(38 mm)

1 ft 6 in
(460 mm)

1¾ in
(45 mm)

8¾ in
(220 mm)

4 Dry-assemble the legs, cross rails, and uprights to make sure that the parts fit together properly, and then check that the frame is perfectly square, using a try square for the inner angles and a straightedge for the diagonal lengths. Make any final adjustments to the mortises and tenons with a ¼ in (6 mm) chisel.

5 Mark out and then cut the 5¾ x 1 in (145 x 25 mm) boards to eight lengths of 1 ft 5⅜ in (441 mm) for the panels. Fit a radiused cutter in a router, and set the depth stop to ¼ in (6 mm). Shape all four edges of each panel so that you produce ¼ in (6 mm) tongues on each edge.

6 Dismantle the dry-assembled frame and cut ¼ x ¼ in (6 x 6 mm) grooves in the inside edges of the cross rails and uprights, to take the panels. Dry-assemble the cross rails and uprights and check that the panels slot into the grooves securely, as they will not be glued during final assembly, to allow for expansion and contraction caused by changing humidity levels.

7 You can either buy four pre-turned 1¾ x 1¾ in (45 x 45 mm) finials or turn them yourself, using a bench lathe or a lathe attachment for an electric drill. Make a template by tracing the finished shape onto a piece of ⅛ in (4 mm) plywood and cutting it out using a jigsaw fitted with a fine scroll blade. Fit a 2⅜ in (60 mm) length of 2 x 2 in (50 x 50 mm) hardwood between the lathe centres and shape it with a skew chisel, checking the shape regularly using the template. Always wear safety goggles when using a lathe.

8 Fit an electric drill onto a sanding table and set the table to an angle of 10°. Sand the top ends of the legs to form shallow pyramids on each one, then drill ¼ in (6 mm) holes ¾ in (19 mm) deep at the peaks of the pyramids and centrally in the four finials. Cut four 1½ in (38 mm) lengths of ¼ in (6 mm) dowel, and glue and fit the dowels into the holes in the legs and finials.

9 Mark out and cut four 1 ft ¼ in (310 mm) lengths of ⅞ x ⅜ in (21 x 10 mm) hardwood for the bearers. Place these along the base of each bottom cross rail and drill three screw holes in each, then screw the bearers in position. Sand all the parts to prepare them for assembly.

10 Apply glue to the joints of two opposite ends of the frame and clamp them using bar clamps. When the glue is dry, glue the other joints and assemble the rest of the frame, holding it with bar clamps and checking that the corners are 90°, using a try square. When the planter is set, cut three 1 ft ¼ in (310 mm) lengths of 4 x ¾ in (100 x 19 mm) hardwood for the bottom supports. Using a ½ in (12 mm) spade bit, drill out four drainage holes on each and lay them across the bearers.

Choosing and Finishing Hardwood

The wood featured in this project is iroko, an imported oily hardwood ideal for exterior use. (Note that its wood dust is very irritating to skin and lungs.) To finish it, liberally apply teak oil, which will provide a weather shield and an attractive sheen (see pp. 74–77). To maintain the protection and the natural color of the wood, reapply the teak oil at least once a year. Other, less oily, hardwoods can be finished using two or three coats of exterior varnish.

LIST OF MATERIALS (*measurements indicate cut size*)

ITEM	SECTION	LENGTH
Hardwood for legs, 4	1¾ x 1¾ in (45 x 45 mm)	6 ft (1840 mm)
Hardwood for cross rails, 8, and uprights, 4	2¾ x ⅞ in (70 x 21 mm)	13 ft 2 in (4000 mm)
Hardwood for finials, 4	1¾ x 1¾ in (45 x 45 mm) diameter	
Hardwood for panels, 8	5¾ x 1 in (145 x 25 mm)	11 ft 7 in (3520 mm)
Hardwood for bearers, 4	⅞ x ⅜ in (21 x 10 mm)	4 ft 1 in (1240 mm)
Hardwood for bottom supports, 3	4 x ¾ in (100 x 19 mm)	3 ft ¾ in (930 mm)
Hardwood dowels, 4	¼ in (6 mm) diameter	6 in (150 mm)
Plated woodscrews		

SIMPLE SEATING

This matching set of bench and chairs uses mortise-and-tenon joints in its construction. The result is an attractive and sturdy set of garden furniture that will provide comfortable seating for years if regularly maintained.

The angled back provides comfortable support.

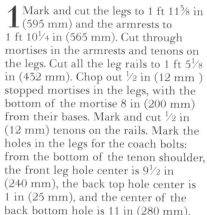

1 Mark and cut the legs to 1 ft 11⅜ in (595 mm) and the armrests to 1 ft 10¼ in (565 mm). Cut through mortises in the armrests and tenons on the legs. Cut all the leg rails to 1 ft 5⅛ in (432 mm). Chop out ½ in (12 mm) stopped mortises in the legs, with the bottom of the mortise 8 in (200 mm) from their bases. Mark and cut ½ in (12 mm) tenons on the rails. Mark the holes in the legs for the coach bolts: from the bottom of the tenon shoulder, the front leg hole center is 9½ in (240 mm), the back top hole center is 1 in (25 mm), and the center of the back bottom hole is 11 in (280 mm).

2 Drill all the holes using a ⁵⁄₁₆ in (9 mm) drill bit. Make two cuts toward the outside of each leg tenon, and glue up the legs, armrests, and leg rails, using one bar clamp across the rail and one more on each armrest and leg joint. Check for square, then carefully drive thin wedges into the cuts in the leg tenons. Cut the six seat frame sides to 1 ft 6¼ in (465 mm), the chair seat frame fronts and backs to 1 ft 7⅝ in (500 mm) and the bench seat frame front and back to 3 ft 7⅜ in (1100 mm).

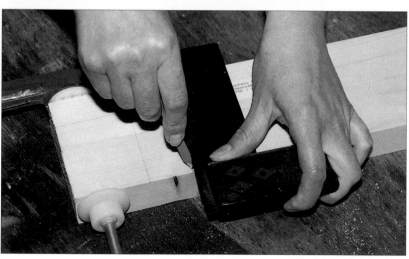

3 Cut the back frame sides to a length of 1 ft 10⅝ in (575 mm), the chair back frame top and bottom rails 1ft 5¾ in (450 mm), and the bench back frame rails 3 ft 7 in (1090 mm). Mark and match the 1⅜ x ½ in (35 x 12 mm) mortise holes in the seat and back side frames: the front and top mortises start at 1⅛ in (30 mm) from the front and top, and the back and bottom ones start at 11¾ in (300 mm) from the end of the first mortises. Chop the mortises to 1½ in (38 mm) deep. Cut out the locating mortises in the top of the seat frame sides, 1¾ in (45 mm) in from the back, and ⁹⁄₁₆ in (14 mm) deep.

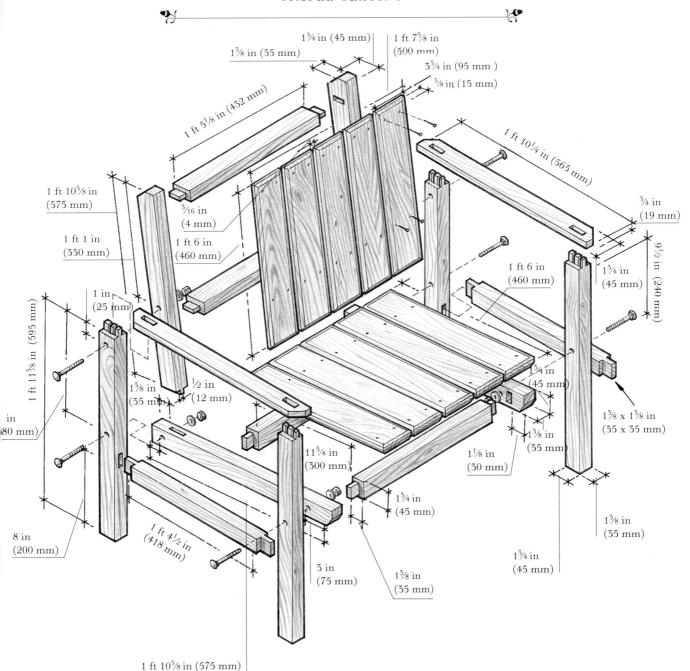

1 3/4 in (45 mm)

1 3/8 in (35 mm)

1 ft 7 5/8 in (500 mm)

3 3/4 in (95 mm)

5/8 in (15 mm)

1 ft 5 1/8 in (432 mm)

1 ft 10 1/4 in (565 mm)

1 ft 10 5/8 in (575 mm)

3/16 in (4 mm)

3/4 in (19 mm)

1 ft 1 in (330 mm)

1 ft 6 in (460 mm)

1 ft 6 in (460 mm)

9 1/2 in (240 mm)

1 3/4 in (45 mm)

1 in (25 mm)

1 ft 11 3/8 in (595 mm)

1 3/8 in (35 mm)

1/2 in (12 mm)

1 3/4 in (45 mm)

1 3/8 x 1 3/8 in (35 x 35 mm)

in 80 mm)

1 3/8 in (35 mm)

11 3/4 in (300 mm)

1 1/8 in (30 mm)

1 3/8 in (35 mm)

8 in (200 mm)

1 ft 4 1/2 in (418 mm)

1 3/4 in (45 mm)

1 3/8 in (35 mm)

1 3/8 in (35 mm)

3 in (75 mm)

1 3/4 in (45 mm)

1 ft 10 5/8 in (575 mm)

4 Cut the tenons on the seat frame fronts and backs and the back frame top and bottom rails to 1½ in (38 mm) deep. Dry-assemble the seat and back frames, checking for square, then glue and clamp them up.

5 Cut all the slats to 1 ft 6 in (460 mm) length, and nail them to the seat and back frames. Work from one side of the frame, leaving a ⅛ in (4 mm) gap between each slat. Use two wire nails at each end of the slats.

6 Mark and cut a 45° angle cut on the top back edge of each back frame side and the lower front edge of each seat frame side. Next, mark and cut a 93° angle for the locating tenon on the back frame sides (see inset). Glue up all the joints on the back frame and seat frame, and clamp them up, ensuring that the angle remains consistent. When dry, assemble the chairs and bench using ⁵⁄₁₆ in (8 mm) coach bolts, washers, and nuts; the slight play through the pre-drilled holes is taken up when the final tightening is made.

Choosing and Treating Wood

The choice of which wood you use for any exterior project often comes down to expense – softwood is cheaper than hardwood, and it can be easier to work with. However, some hardwoods require less exterior treatment and maintenance. Whatever you choose, always check the timber before you purchase to make sure that the wood is of good quality, free of splits, uneven grain, and knots, and that it does not twist or bow along its length. Most defects can be detected by looking down a length of wood, and by checking the end section for distortion.

Wood with few defects in this area is usually graded as "firsts" or "firsts and seconds" (FAS) quality. Using cheap wood cannot guarantee the same results as with more carefully chosen, if more expensive, materials. If you use reclaimed wood for its stability and weathered appearance, you will have to live with any defects – however, any teething troubles will have long since been resolved.

For a long-lasting finish, it is best to treat all the parts of the furniture before assembling the seats and bench. The legs can be stood in bowls of preservative, while the other parts can be brushed and left to dry. When using preservative, follow the manufacturer's instructions. After that, the choice of finish is up to you (see also the Finishing section, pp. 74–77).

LIST OF MATERIALS (*measurements indicate cut size*)		
BASIC STRUCTURE	**SECTION**	**LENGTH**
Softwood for legs, 12	1¾ x 1⅜ in (45 x 35 mm)	23 ft 4½ in (7140 mm)
Softwood for armrests, 6	1¾ x ¾ in (45 x 19 mm)	11 ft 1½ in (3390 mm)
Softwood for leg rails, 6	1⅜ x 1⅜ in (35 x 35 mm)	8 ft 6¾ in (2592 mm)
Softwood for slats, 42	3¾ x ¾ in (95 x 19 mm)	63 ft (19 m 320 mm)
SEAT FRAME Softwood for sides, 6	1¾ x 1⅜ in (45 x 35 mm)	9 ft 1½ in (2790 mm)
Softwood for fronts, 3, and backs, 3	1¾ x 1⅜ in (45 x 35 mm)	13 ft 9 in (4200 mm)
BACK FRAME Softwood for sides, 6	1¾ x 1⅜ in (45 x 35 mm)	11 ft 3¾ in (3450 mm)
Softwood for top rails, 3, and bottom rails, 3	1¾ x 1⅜ in (45 x 35 mm)	13 ft 1 in (3980 mm)
Coach bolts, nuts, and washers, 18	5⁄16 in (8 mm) diameter	3 in (75 mm)
Bright wire nails		

FOLDAWAY HERB PLANTER

This planter has separate lift-out boxes for a variety of herbs. The top tray can be removed from the legs and the lower shelf is hinged so that the planter can be stored away when not in use.

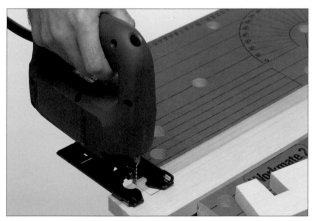

1 Mark out and cut the tray sides to 2 ft 9¾ in (860 mm) length and tray ends to 1 ft 3¾ in (400 mm). Mark 1 in (25 mm) edge-to-edge half-lap joints with their centers 3½ in (90 mm) from the ends, on the bottom edge and top edge of the sides, and cut out the waste. Mark and cut a 12° angle from the top end of each piece.

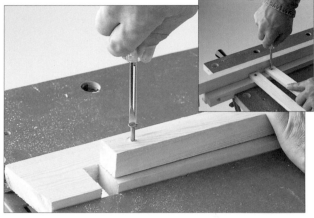

2 Assemble the frame. Cut the side bearers to 2 ft 2 in (660 mm) and glue and screw them along the tray sides, ½ in (12 mm) from the bottom edge. Cut and fix the 6 in (150 mm) end bearers. Cut the slats to 8 in (200 mm). Glue and screw the first to the end and side bearers (see inset), then the others, leaving ¾ in (19 mm) gaps.

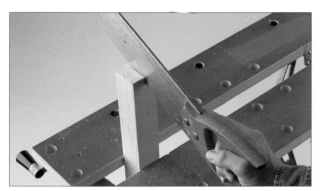

3 Cut the legs to 2 ft 6 in (760 mm) length, and saw out a 3 x 1 in (75 x 25 mm) rabbet at the top of each leg. Mark and cut the cross rails to 8 in (200 mm) length and glue and screw them into the rabbets, checking the legs are square. Cut four locating blocks for the legs and fix to the inside corners of the tray bottom.

4 Mark and cut the shelf sides to 1 ft 10 in (560 mm) length and the ends to 6 in (150 mm) length. Drill dowel holes in the end grain of the ends and matching holes in the inside faces of the sides, and glue in dowels. Assemble and clamp the shelf frame. Cut the shelf bearer sides to 1 ft 10 in (560 mm) length and bearer ends to 4 in (100 mm), and assemble as for the tray bearers. Cut 14 slats to 6 in (150 mm) length and fix to the bearers as before.

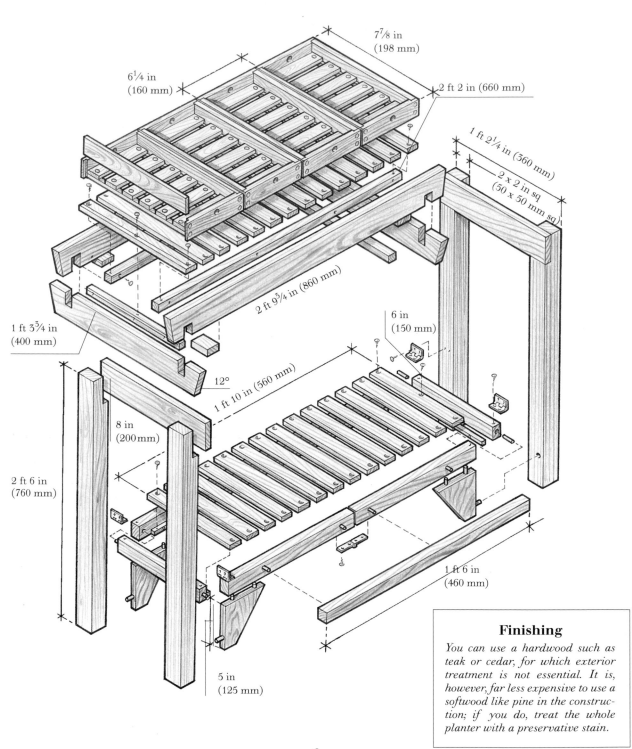

7⅞ in (198 mm)

6¼ in (160 mm)

2 ft 2 in (660 mm)

1 ft 2¼ in (360 mm)

2 x 2 in sq (50 x 50 mm sq)

2 ft 9¾ in (860 mm)

6 in (150 mm)

1 ft 3¾ in (400 mm)

12°

1 ft 10 in (560 mm)

8 in (200mm)

2 ft 6 in (760 mm)

1 ft 6 in (460 mm)

5 in (125 mm)

Finishing

You can use a hardwood such as teak or cedar, for which exterior treatment is not essential. It is, however, far less expensive to use a softwood like pine in the construction; if you do, treat the whole planter with a preservative stain.

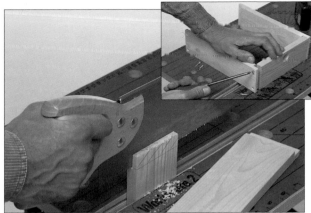

5 Cut the shelf braces to 5 in (125 mm) length and shape as shown. Drill dowel holes in the top edges and in the shelf sides, staggering them so that the leg assembly and shelf can fold up. Drill one dowel hole in each brace side edge and glue to the shelf sides. Insert dowels on the brace side edges and mark and drill matching dowel holes in the legs. Cut the shelf sides at the halfway point, and screw backflap hinges onto their bottom edges. With the brace dowels placed in their leg holes, screw in the backflap hinges to fix the shelf to the legs.

6 Cut the stabilizer bar to 1 ft 6 in (460 mm) length, and drill and insert dowels along it. Drill matching dowel holes in the outside edge of one shelf side. Assemble the legs and tray and fit the bar in place. Next, cut the eight box sides to $7\frac{7}{8}$ in (198 mm) and the eight front and backs to $6\frac{1}{4}$ in (160 mm). Drill finger holes in the fronts and backs, then cut 1 in (25 mm) rebates at both ends of the sides (see above). Glue and screw the boxes together (see inset), then cut the eight side bearers to $5\frac{7}{8}$ in (148 mm) length and the eight front and back bearers to $2\frac{3}{8}$ in (60 mm). Fix these as described before, then cut sixteen slats to $4\frac{1}{4}$ in (110 mm) length, and fit four to each box.

LIST OF MATERIALS (*measurements indicate cut size*)

ITEM	SECTION	LENGTH
Hardwood/softwood for tray sides, 2, and ends, 2	3 x 1 in (75 x 25 mm)	8 ft 3 in (2520 mm)
Hardwood/softwood for bearers for box, 16, shelf, 4, tray, 4	1 x 1 in (25 x 25 mm)	15 ft 2 in (4604 mm)
Hardwood/softwood for legs, 4	2 x 2 in (50 x 50 mm)	10 ft (3040 mm)
Hardwood/softwood for cross rails, 2	3 x 1 in (75 x 25 mm)	1 ft 4 in (406 mm)
Hardwood/softwood for slats for top, 14, shelf, 14, boxes, 16	1 x $\frac{1}{2}$ in (25 x 12 mm)	22 ft (6660 mm)
Hardwood/softwood for shelf sides, 2, ends, 2, stabilizer bar	$1\frac{1}{2}$ x 1 in (38 x 25 mm)	6 ft 2 in (1880 mm)
Hardwood/softwood for box sides, 8, and front and backs, 8	3 x 1 in (75 x 25 mm)	9 ft 5 in (2864 mm)
Plywood for shelf braces, 4	5 x $\frac{1}{2}$ in (125 x 12 mm)	1 ft 8 in (500 mm)
Softwood doweling	$\frac{3}{8}$ in (10 mm) diameter	3 ft $3\frac{1}{2}$ in (1000 mm)
Backflap hinges, 6		1 in (25 mm)
No. 8 woodscrews		1 in (25 mm)

WHEELBARROW PLANTER

This project is an ideal way to use up offcuts, waste wood or exterior-grade plywood. Because it will probably be filled with soil and plants, there is no real need to plane or saw everything exactly.

1 The sides, ends and bottom are made from narrow boards edge-jointed together. Plane each over-length board flat, then put one piece in a vice and spread glue along its edge. Take the other board and rub its edge back and forth to ensure that the glue works into the grain. Remove from the vice and place in bar clamps.

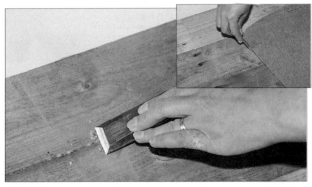

2 Make the wheel up from two thicknesses, with the grain in opposing directions. Plane the two adjoining faces flat, as well as the edges. Spread plenty of glue over one face and clamp up. When dry, clean off any excess with a chisel. Make templates for all components except for the bottom of the box. With each of the sets of boards glued up, trace the templates carefully (see inset).

3 Mark out the wheel to 9½ in (240 mm) diameter, then mark out and drill out the central hole to a diameter of 1⅛ in (30 mm), working from both sides. The holes in the handles need to be oversize to accommodate the shaft going through at an angle, so use a 1¼ in (32 mm) drill bit and cant the hole slightly.

4 Cut each of the components out by hand or on a bandsaw. Bevel each of the small shaped supports on the adjacent face to the box, at an angle of around 85°.

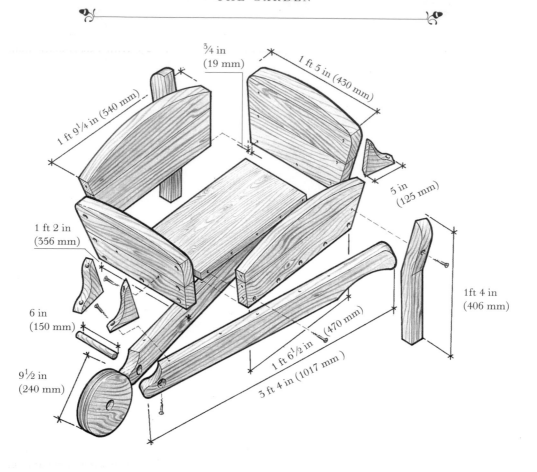

LIST OF MATERIALS *(measurements indicate cut size)*		
ITEM	**SECTION**	**LENGTH**
Wood for arms, 2	3 x 1¼ in (75 x 32 mm)	6 ft 8 in (2034 mm)
Wood for legs, 2	3 x 1½ in (75 x 38 mm)	2 ft 8 in (812 mm)
Wood for sides, 2	8 x 1 in (200 x 25 mm)	3 ft 6½ in (1080 mm)
Wood for ends, 2	9½ x 1 in (240 x 25 mm)	2 ft 10 in (860 mm)
Wood for support blocks, 4	4 x 1 in (100 x 25 mm)	1 ft 8 in (500 mm)
Wood for bottom, 1	¾ x 1 in (19 x 25 mm)	11½ in (293 mm)
Wood for shaft, 1	1 in (25 mm) diameter	6 in (150 mm)
Wood for wheel, 1	1¼ in (32 mm)	9½ in (240 mm) diameter
Chipboard screws	1¾ in (45 mm) diameter	

Finishing

For a roughly constructed project such as this, either treat it with a preservative and woodstain (see p. 76), or paint it in bright, primary colors. Renew the finish annually.

6 With a spokeshave, router rasp or file, smooth any exposed areas. Put the box together, using a ³/₄ in (19 mm) spacer strip to set the sides in from the ends. When fixing into end grain, use 1³/₄ in (45 mm) chipboard screws and plenty of glue. Bevel back the lower edge of the bottom to make a good fit, then fix in place with plenty of glue and screws again. Plane the bottom front and back edges of the box reasonably level with the bottom, to provide a flat platform for the arms to fit snugly up to the bottom.

7 Turn the box over and set out the positions for the handles. The gap between the handles at the back is 8¹/₂ in (215 mm), and 3¹/₄ in (83 mm) at the front. Place the handles on, with the noses protruding about 7 in (178 mm) in front. Mark the positions on the bottom and remove the handles. Drill up from the bottom pilot holes through each of the base boards, then turn them over and countersink them. Position the handles with plenty of glue on the top edge, place the box on top, and screw into position. Cut the shaft to 6 in (150 mm) length. Drill a couple of holes up from the bottom of the shaft holes.

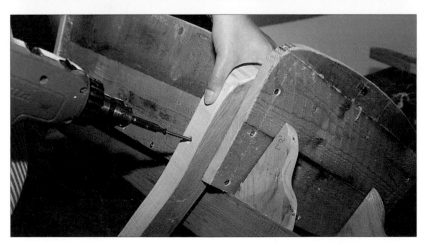

8 Position the wheel between the noses, thread the shaft, and fix in place. Pre-drill and countersink the box support brackets and fix them in place. Set the legs slightly lower than the top of the box and flush up against the overhang. Check the angle of the tilt, then fix them in place with plenty of glue and screw from both sides.

STOWAWAY PICNIC TABLE

The top of this stylish table can be removed and the legs folded straight for easy storage. It can be made from a domestic or imported hardwood; soft-wood must be treated with preservative.

The legs fit inside the table top underframe.

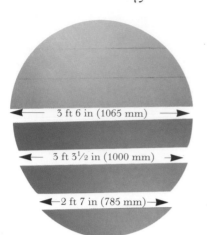

1 Mark out a semicircular template on ½ in (12 mm) MDF, with the straight edge 3 ft 6 in (1065 mm) long and a radius of 1 ft 9 in (535 mm). Mark two lines across at 6⅞ in (175 mm) intervals, and cut along these lines. This will produce two pieces 3 ft 6 in (1065 mm) long at the longest point, two at 3 ft 3½ in (1000 mm) and two at 2 ft 7 in (785 mm).

2 Use the templates to mark the shapes onto timber, and use a jigsaw to cut out the six table top pieces. To make a jig, fix screws through the MDF pieces into the timber, and trim all the edges with a straight cutter in a router. Fit a ⅛ in (4 mm) roundover cutter, and round over all the timber edges.

3 Cut the six underframe pieces to 1 ft 8¾ in (528 mm). Use an adjustable bevel to mark a 60° angle at each end, with the shorter marks on the same face. Cut the angles on each piece using a tenon saw.

4 Use a marking gauge to set out the joints on the underframe pieces. On one end of each piece, mark out a central tenon 1 1/16 in (27 mm) wide and with shoulders of the same measurement, working from the long edge of the cut angle. On the other end, mark a central slot 1 1/16 in (27 mm) wide and the same distance deep, again working from the long edge of the cut angle.

5 Cut out the tenons on each end using a tenon saw, keeping to the waste side of the marked line. Use a coping saw to cut out the slots on the other end, and chisel out the bottom of each joint. Dry-assemble the pieces to make a hexagon, checking each joint for fit, and number the matching ends. Position the hexagon on a sheet of 12 mm (½ in) MDF and mark out the interior shape. Remove the underframe pieces and cut out the shape, cutting small access cut-outs at the joint angles.

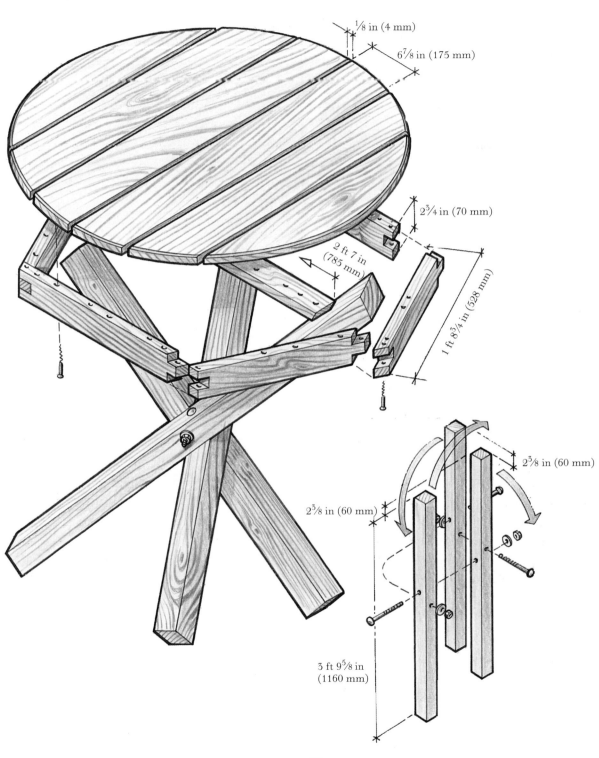

1/8 in (4 mm)

6 7/8 in (175 mm)

2 3/4 in (70 mm)

2 ft 7 in
(785 mm)

1 ft 8 3/4 in (528 mm)

2 3/8 in (60 mm)

2 3/8 in (60 mm)

3 ft 9 5/8 in
(1160 mm)

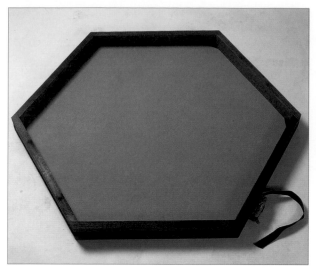

6 Apply glue to the joints and reassemble the under-frame around the MDF board, ensuring that you correctly match the numbered ends. Hold the underframe tightly in shape with a web clamp, and check that each joint fits snugly.

7 Mark and drill a screw hole through each joint, and insert a $\frac{1}{4}$ x $2\frac{3}{8}$ in (6 x 60 mm) countersunk woodscrew to hold the joint tightly.

8 Position the table top pieces face down, using five $\frac{1}{8}$ in (4 mm) plywood strips as spacers between them. Lay the underframe in position on the top and drill four countersunk screw holes through each underframe piece, ensuring that the holes go into the underside of the table top. Use $\frac{1}{4}$ x $2\frac{3}{8}$ in (6 x 60 mm) countersunk woodscrews to fix the underframe tightly to the table top.

9 Cut a center bearer to 2 ft 7 in (785 mm), and mark and cut 60° angles on the ends in the same manner as for the underframe pieces. Position the bearer so that it lies across each table top piece, then drill two countersunk screw holes for the four inner pieces, and one for each outer piece. Use $\frac{1}{4}$ x $1\frac{3}{8}$ in (6 x 35 mm) countersunk woodscrews to fix the bearer tightly to the table top.

10 Cut the legs to 3 ft 9⅝ in (1160 mm), and square off and mark the top of each one. Position the legs together and mark a central drill hole 1 ft 9⅝ in (550 mm) from the top on each face, and a similar central hole 1 ft 9⅝ in (550 mm) from the bottom on each side. Drill the holes through each leg using a ⅜ in (10 mm) bit. Following the diagram on p. 71, place the face of one leg against the side of another with the top of the first leg 2⅜ in (60 mm) below the other, and tap a coach bolt through the first leg top hole and fit a washer and nut. Place the face edge of the third leg to the side edge of the first leg, with its top 2⅜ in (60 mm) below that of the first leg. Tap a coach bolt through the third leg top hole and the first leg bottom hole as before. Screw the third coach bolt through the top hole of the second leg. With legs opened and placed against the bolts, fit the top of the legs inside the underframe.

Woods and Finishing

Using hardwood to construct the Stowaway table is ideal, but choose the wood with care. Bear in mind that teak is very expensive, and working iroko can be hazardous to your health. Native hardwoods, such as oak and beech, are also suitable.

If you intend to work with softwood for this project, each component should be treated prior to assembly with preservative. When applying protective varnish, make sure that you treat all the undersurfaces, particularly areas such as the bottoms of the legs.

LIST OF MATERIALS (*measurements indicate cut size*)

ITEM	SECTION	LENGTH
MDF for top template, 1	1 ft 9 in x ½ in (535 x 12 mm)	3 ft 6 in (1065 mm)
Hardwood/treated softwood for table top, 6	6⅞ x ¾ in (175 x 20 mm)	18 ft 9 in (5700 mm)
Hardwood/treated softwood for center bearer, 1	2¼ x ¾ in (55 x 20 mm)	2 ft 7 in (785 mm)
Hardwood/treated softwood for underframe, 6	2¾ x 1 in (70 x 25 mm)	10 ft 4½ in (3168 mm)
Hardwood/treated softwood for legs, 3	2⅜ x 2⅜ in (60 x 60 mm)	11 ft 4⅞ in (3480 mm)
Countersunk zinc woodscrews for underframe, 30	¼ in (6 mm) diameter	2⅜ in (60 mm)
Countersunk zinc woodscrews for bearer, 10	¼ in (6 mm) diameter	1⅜ in (35 mm)
Black or galvanized coach bolts, nuts, and washers, 3	5⁄16 in (8 mm) diameter	5⅛ in (130 mm)

COMBATING THE ELEMENTS

You should coat all projects with a finish, to enhance the appearance of the timber as well as to protect it — this is particularly necessary with garden and outdoor projects, where weather conditions can quickly spoil untreated timber. There are many specialized finishes available, ranging from preservatives to natural oils.

Vandyke crystals
The crystals are mixed with water to create a rich color (see p. 76).

Oil-based woodstain
Usually available in brown wood colors, oil-based stains penetrate the wood and tend to run easily along the grain.

Water-based varnish
Water-based, or acrylic, varnish is generally white in color and washes off brushes after use.

Weatherproofing

There are two main issues to be dealt with when conserving timber outdoors: protecting existing woodwork and incorporating design details which ensure that new exterior and garden projects will last.

Essentially, wood needs to be protected from moisture, biological attack, and sunlight. Moisture affects timber primarily by causing splitting and loss of adhesion — these are the results of the existing moisture content of "dried" timber, rather than rainfall. Moisture also contributes to biological decay, as it is an essential ingredient for bacterial and fungal agents to flourish; these generally need more than 22 percent moisture content to become active, and once they do, remedial action is essential, as well as preventative treatment for the future.

Sunlight, or more specifically UV (ultraviolet) light, has a damaging effect on most surfaces that are exposed to it. Sunlight can bleach exposed timber and degrade the surface, even more so when moisture is present. Another effect of the sun is that it heats surface temperatures sufficiently to further split timber and cause resin to be exuded. This affects dark timber finishes significantly more, for example, than white painted wood.

Designing for Longevity

Always consider the combined effect of moisture, biological attack, and sunlight when working on the design of joinery details. The aim is to keep the item as dry as possible throughout its working life, while at the same time providing the best possible surface to which protective coatings can adhere.

Starting with the types of joint that are likely to be used for exterior projects — windows, doors, garden furniture, planters, arbors, and so on — the mortise-and-tenon joint is a prevalent feature. Although it is a strong joint, it will in time provide a direct route for water to penetrate into the heart of the timber. This is usually shortly after the glue in the joint loses adhesion to the timber's surface or eventually breaks down completely. No glue lasts forever, if only because of the amount of movement the timber around it is likely to undergo through the seasons.

Wedging tenons in the traditional manner should help to keep joints tight, but dipping the components in a preservative before assembly — and preferably soaking them overnight — gives even better protection. Similarly, keep the outer coating of varnish or paint intact, and don't wait until peeling is well advanced before retreating it.

Just as important as keeping water out is letting water escape from timber, particularly from windows, where condensation can be a problem. Just because rain can't get to it doesn't necessarily mean that it will remain dry; remember that the continued presence of moisture is a key ingredient in causing decay.

Rails and Sills

Because it is more than likely that rails and sills will be subjected to driving rain at some time in the year, making them shed rain and resist penetration at their openings requires careful detailing. The best-known feature is the "drip" found on sills and rails: this keeps water from flowing down and under the wood, back to the wall, by providing a break line. This can easily be routed into the bottom of the rail or sill, using a radius cutter; capillary grooves are also effective in keeping water from blowing through, and these can be routed using a bearing-guided slotter. Surfaces should be angled at least 10°, and you can also cut a second rabbet to create a stepped surface; this prevents water on a sill from being blown back into a casement window opening.

Another method of increasing longevity is to use hardwood or pressure-treated softwood in construction, providing an extra front line of defense. Hardwood also has the advantage of superior mechanical strength, resisting knocks and abrasions — exactly the kind of injury suffered by sills and rails, particularly at ground level.

Surface Preparation

Just because it is outdoors doesn't mean it shouldn't be smooth. Microscopic analysis suggests that imperfections in the surface of timber can lead to much thinner adhesion on small ridges and bumps, which effectively means that little or no undercoat or first coat may adhere; places where this occurs are the obvious starting points for peeling or other degradation. Similarly, all edges should be radiused to a minimum of ⅛ in (4 mm) to help coating adhere, and timber that has already been damaged by exposure to sun and rain should be sanded down to good wood before further treatment begins.

When it comes to choosing timber for a project, moisture content is critical, whether you use hardwood or softwood.

Sealing knots
Before painting timber, seal any "live" knots that seep resin by brushing on one thin layer of wood sealer, which is a shellac-based sealant.

Staining end grain
With the end grain held horizontally, use a stipple action to make sure that the stain gets absorbed deeply into the timber.

Spreading stain evenly
Work quickly and evenly over each face to be stained, and brush out any puddles or runs as soon as they form.

Making woodstain
*Vandyke crystals are easy to prepare and use. Combine
1 part crystals with 5 parts warm water and mix well
(use more water for a lighter shade and less water for
a darker one).*

Applying stain
*Brush on a generous layer of stain to the wood. Do not
allow it to dry in between strokes, since any overlap may
create darker areas.*

Wiping off stain
*Use a clean dry cloth to wipe off excess stain, and allow the
stain to dry naturally. Vandyke crystals can stain skin and
nails, so always wear protective gloves.*

A wood with a moisture content above 20 percent may
become problematic when allowed to air-dry further, but
overly dry timber (for example, 8 percent kiln-dried for
interior use) will also cause any surface treatment to crack.

Coatings

What used to be called paint, varnish, or oil is now known
as a coating. However, there are more differences than
simply a change in name. Where ranges of exterior varnish
were once limited to certain types of solvent-based
products, and paint was either alkyd or oil-based gloss,
attempts to develop environmentally viable and user-
friendly coatings have led to a leap forward, particularly
where acrylic-based finishes are concerned.

Which finish to use is never an easy decision, although
your choice may be conditioned by a color requirement.
Perhaps the simplest way to categorize the various finishes
available is to say that the most durable ones inevitably let
less of the character of the wood show through. This may
not be a major issue in exterior projects, but if you use
hardwood in garden furniture, you might prefer a finer and
more easily renewable finish.

Many finishes work best outdoors when they are preceded
by a preservative, even though the finish may also contain
a fungicide. It is worth using a preservative because
fungicides are most effective when they penetrate the
timber as deeply as possible, either by pressure treatment or
by overnight soaking. Take great care when using
preservatives, since they are often very thin — like water —
which makes them good for soaking into end grain, but just
as effective at penetrating gloves and protective clothing.

Woodstains

Replacing or supplementing traditional paint finishes with
colored woodstains is also high on the agenda of
manufacturers; these are developed for situations where a
colored finish is required, but eliminate the need for
elaborate priming, undercoating, and top coating. One of
the great advantages of any pigmented coating, whether
paint or woodstain, is that the pigment acts as an effective
absorber of UV light, exceeding the capacity of the UV
absorbers that are added to clear varnishes.

Woodstains also allow some of the wood's character to show through. The aim is usually to make application as simple and rapid as possible, while providing a "breathable" finish; this prevents the problem of an apparently effective top coat hiding the fact that it has lost surface adhesion and is masking damp wood beneath, which can gradually rot until the paint finally flakes off. While a degree of breathability is a good thing, particularly on rough-sawn exterior timber where dimensional stability isn't necessarily critical, in joinery projects the finish needs to minimize the amount of movement in the timber through all the seasons of the year. It is also necessary to find a balance in providing sufficient elasticity in the coating to cope with moisture movement and to resist cracking.

Acrylic Finishes

Available for both exterior and interior use, acrylic finishes are environmentally friendly reinventions of polyurethane varnishes. They perform well and bring a number of major benefits to the user. Because they are water-based, there is little odor during application, and brushes can be cleaned with water after use. Acrylics are milky when wet, drying to a clear finish, so that you can see when they are dry. Finally, acrylics have a quick drying time, usually touch-dry within an hour and recoatable within around four hours. The durability of acrylics is excellent, lasting for five years or more before refinishing is necessary, depending on location and conditions.

"Natural" Finishes

This heading covers oil finishes such as teak oil, Danish oil (see top right), and tung oil, that give a more natural effect and can be used both externally and internally. While providing some but not all of the sealing and protective qualities of the other finishes described here, their main strength out of doors lies in their being easy to apply again and again, which means that timber can be treated regularly with a minimum of preparation (one recent development is spray-on teak oil). The beautiful natural finish allows the wood to age gracefully and develop a natural patina, which works particularly well on quality garden furniture made from hardwood.

Danish oil on oak
Danish oil resists water and seals the wood pores, preventing the wood from becoming dirty. It is also useful for revitalizing old timber.

Tinted varnish on hemlock
Tinted varnish has the same qualities as clear varnish (see below), and colors the wood at the same time. The more coats you apply, the darker the finish.

Clear varnish on cherry
Varnish protects wood from scratches, heat marks, and moisture penetration. Exterior-grade varnish is best for outdoor projects.

Colored preservative on redwood
A colored preservative enables you to stain and protect the timber using just one project. The "deep-penetrating" varieties give the best protection.

Oil-based stain on redwood
This stains colored wood, but does not protect it. You can buy proprietary stains or make up your own (see opposite); water-based stains are more environmentally friendly.

INDEX

ACKNOWLEDGMENTS

Makers

Bob Piper (Channel Rye Ltd): Versailles Planter (p. 10),
Octagonal Table (p. 20), Garden Shed (p. 36).
Mark Ramuz: Birdhouse (p. 16).
Frank Delicata: Square Planter (p. 48).
Peter Bishop: Garden Trug (p. 26), Simple Seating (p. 54),
Wheelbarrow Planter (p. 64).
James Summers (Pearl Dot Ltd): Pine Arbor (p. 42).
Steve Hounslow/James Summers (Pearl Dot Ltd):
Stowaway Picnic Table (p. 68).

Suppliers

Stowaway Picnic Table (p. 68): Metal chair
courtesy of The Pier, London.

Photographers

Geoff Dann: pp. 8, 36, 68, 75–77.
Sampson Lloyd: pp. 27, 29, 37, 39–40, 54–55, 64, 69, 70, 72–73.
John Freeman: pp. 42–43, 45–46, 60, 61, 63.